# Taking Care Of You
# A Simple Guide To Self-Care

*Olivia Garcia*

ISBN: 9798373598620

# Contents

# Introduction To Self-Care

Self-care is the practice of taking care of oneself in order to maintain physical, emotional, and mental well-being. It encompasses a wide range of activities and behaviors that contribute to overall health and happiness.

Self-care is important for everyone, as it can help prevent burnout, stress, and other negative effects of a hectic and demanding lifestyle. By making self-care a priority, individuals can improve their physical and mental health, increase their productivity and effectiveness, and create a more balanced and fulfilling life.

Self-care can be divided into several different categories, such as physical self-care, emotional self-care, mental self-care, social self-care, spiritual self-care, financial self-care, and occupational self-care. Each category focuses on different aspects of well-being and includes a variety of activities and behaviors that can be tailored to the individual's needs.

Some examples of self-care activities include exercise, healthy eating, getting enough sleep, practicing mindfulness, journaling, talking to a therapist, setting goals, spending time with friends and family, and finding time for leisure activities.

Self-care is not a one-time thing, it's a habit. It's important to make self-care a regular part of daily life in order to see the long-term benefits. This may mean setting aside specific time each day for self-care activities, or incorporating self-care into daily routines.

In this book, we will explore various aspects of self-care in depth, provide tips and strategies for incorporating self-care into daily life, and discuss ways to make self-care a sustainable habit. By the end of this book, you will have a greater understanding of the importance of self-care and the various ways in which it can improve your overall well-being.

# Physical Self-Care

Physical self-care is the practice of taking care of one's body in order to maintain overall health and well-being. This includes activities such as exercise, healthy eating, getting enough sleep, and managing stress. By making physical self-care a priority, individuals can improve their physical health, increase their energy levels, and reduce their risk of chronic diseases.

Exercise: Regular exercise is an important part of physical self-care. It can improve cardiovascular health, help control weight, and reduce the risk of chronic diseases such as diabetes and heart disease. The U.S. Department of Health and Human Services recommends at least 150 minutes of moderate-intensity aerobic activity or 75 minutes of vigorous-intensity aerobic activity per week, and muscle-strengthening activities on at least 2 days a week.

Nutrition: Eating a healthy diet is another important aspect of physical self-care. A balanced diet should include a variety of nutrient-dense foods, such as fruits, vegetables, whole grains, lean protein, and healthy fats. In addition, it's important to limit the intake of processed foods, sugary drinks, and saturated fats. A healthy diet can provide energy and help reduce the risk of chronic diseases.

Sleep: Getting enough quality sleep is crucial for physical self-care. Poor sleep can lead to a host of health problems, including weight gain, anxiety, and depression. The National Sleep Foundation recommends adults get between 7 and 9 hours of sleep per night.

Stress management: Stress can take a toll on the body, so managing it is important for physical self-care. Some effective ways to manage stress include exercise, yoga, meditation, and deep breathing exercises. Getting enough sleep, eating a healthy diet, and limiting the intake of caffeine and alcohol can also help reduce stress levels.

It's important to remember that physical self-care is not only important for adults but also for children and adolescents. encouraging good habits early in life can lead to healthier and more fulfilling lives.

It's important to find an exercise routine that works for you, and to make it a regular part of your routine. Whether it's going to the gym, running, cycling, swimming, or taking a yoga class, the key is to find something that you enjoy and can stick to. The same goes for healthy eating, finding a diet that works for you and you can stick to is key.

Incorporating physical self-care into daily life can be challenging, but it is worth it. By making physical self-care a priority, individuals can improve their physical health, increase their energy levels, and reduce their risk of chronic diseases.

Here are a few quotes related to physical self-care:

"The body is the temple of the soul and it's our responsibility to take care of it." – Unknown

"Take care of your body, it's the only place you have to live." - Jim Rohn

"Eat well, sleep well, move well, breathe well. These are the pillars of well-being." -Dr. Habib Sadeghi

"Physical fitness is not only one of the most important keys to a healthy body, it is the basis of dynamic and creative intellectual activity." - John F. Kennedy

"Exercise is a powerful antidepressant and mood elevating agent." – Unknown

"The greatest wealth is to live
content with little." – Plato

"Physical activity is the single most powerful tool we have to optimize our brain function." - John Ratey, MD

"Healthy citizens are the greatest asset any country can have." - Winston Churchill

"The miracle isn't that I finished. The miracle is that I had the courage to start." - John Bingham, marathon runner

"Your body can stand almost anything. It's your mind that you have to convince." – Unknown

These quotes remind us the importance of taking care of our physical body and how it's important to keep it healthy and strong to have an overall well-being.

# Emotional Self-Care

Emotional self-care is the practice of taking care of one's emotional well-being in order to maintain overall health and happiness. It involves managing and processing emotions in a healthy way, and includes activities such as journaling, mindfulness, therapy, and positive self-talk. By making emotional self-care a priority, individuals can improve their emotional intelligence, gain insight into their emotions, and increase their capacity for empathy and understanding.

Journaling: Writing about one's thoughts and feelings can be a powerful tool for emotional self-care. It allows individuals to process their emotions, gain insight into their thoughts, and identify patterns in their behavior. Journaling can also help reduce feelings of stress and anxiety and increase feelings of gratitude and positive self-talk.

Mindfulness: Mindfulness is the practice of being present in the moment, without judgment. It can help individuals become more aware of their thoughts and feelings, and gain perspective on them. Mindfulness can be practiced through meditation, deep breathing exercises, or other activities such as yoga.

Therapy: Talking to a therapist or counselor can be a powerful tool for emotional self-care. A therapist can help individuals work through difficult emotions, gain insight into their behavior, and develop coping strategies for dealing with stress and other challenges.

Positive self-talk: Our inner thoughts and dialogue can have a huge impact on our emotions and mood. Emphasizing positive thoughts and emotions, and challenging negative thoughts can be helpful to change the way we feel and react.

It's important to note that self-care does not mean completely avoiding or ignoring negative emotions, as it's important to face and process them. However, it's about finding a balance and knowing when to take a step back, process, and care for oneself.

It's important to find a routine that works for you, and to make it a regular part of your day. Whether it's journaling for five minutes in the morning, practicing mindfulness during lunch, or talking to a therapist once a week, the key is to find something that you enjoy and can stick to.

Incorporating emotional self-care into daily life can be challenging, but it is worth it. By making emotional self-care a priority, individuals can improve their emotional intelligence, gain insight into their emotions, and increase their capacity for empathy and understanding.

Here are a few quotes related to emotional self-care:

"The most powerful relationship you will ever have is the relationship with yourself." -Steve Maraboli

"You can't pour from an empty cup. Take care of yourself first." – Unknown

"Emotional pain is not something that should be hidden away and never spoken about. It is a part of the human experience that needs to be acknowledged and processed in a healthy way." –unknown

"Emotional self-care means giving ourselves permission to feel, and to then process and move on from those feelings." -Cleo Wade

"Emotional intelligence is the ability to recognize our own feelings and those of others, and to manage emotions in ourselves and in our relationships." -Daniel Goleman

"Self-care is never a selfish act—it is simply good stewardship of the only gift I have, the gift I was put on earth to offer to others." - Parker Palmer

"Emotional healing is not about forgetting the past, but about accepting and learning from it." – Unknown

"Self-care is not about perfection; it's about simplicity, consistency, and doing the best you can." – Unknown

"Caring for myself is not self-indulgence, it is self-preservation, and that is an act of political warfare." - Audre Lorde

"You yourself, as much as anybody in the entire universe, deserve your love and affection." –Buddha

These quotes remind us the importance of emotional self-care, how it is essential to have a healthy emotional life, and how it's important to take care of our emotional well-being in order to have an overall well-being. It also highlights the importance of self-compassion and self-love.

# Mental Self-Care

Mental self-care is the practice of taking care of one's mental health and well-being in order to maintain overall health and happiness. It involves developing healthy coping mechanisms and building resilience to deal with stress, and includes activities such as cognitive-behavioral therapy, goal setting, and stress management. By making mental self-care a priority, individuals can improve their mental health, increase their productivity, and develop a more positive outlook on life.

Cognitive-behavioral therapy (CBT): CBT is a form of psychotherapy that helps individuals identify and change negative thought patterns and behaviors. It can be helpful in managing stress, anxiety, depression, and other mental health issues.

Goal setting: Setting and working towards goals can be a powerful tool for mental self-care. It can help individuals feel a sense of purpose and direction, and give them a sense of accomplishment and satisfaction.

Stress management: Stress can have a negative impact on mental health, so it's important to manage it effectively. Some effective ways to manage stress include exercise, mindfulness, deep breathing, and spending time outdoors.

Resilience building: Resilience is the ability to recover from adversity and bounce back from challenges. Building resilience can help individuals become more resilient in the face of stress and life challenges. This could include activities such as volunteering, practicing gratitude and learning to accept failure as part of the process.

It's also important to remember that mental self-care is not just about treating mental health issues, but also about maintaining good mental health by adopting preventive measures.

It's important to find a routine that works for you, and to make it a regular part of your day. Whether it's going to therapy, setting daily goals, or taking a walk outside, the key is to find something that you enjoy and can stick to.

Incorporating mental self-care into daily life can be challenging, but it is worth it. By making mental self-care a priority, individuals can improve their mental health, increase their productivity, and develop a more positive outlook on life.

Here are a few quotes related to mental self-care:

"The mind is everything; what you think you become." – Buddha

"The greatest weapon against stress is our ability to choose one thought over another." -William James

"The mind is a powerful tool. If you fill it with positive thoughts, your life will start to change." –Unknown

"The only way to do great work is to love what you do. If you haven't found it yet, keep looking." - Steve Jobs

"The more that you read, the more things you will know. The more that you learn, the more places you'll go." -Dr. Seuss

"The first step to mental wellness is understanding that your thoughts aren't facts." – Unknown

"A healthy mind requires a healthy body." –Unknown

"The best way to predict your future is to create it." – Abraham Lincoln

"Change the way you look at things
and the things you look at change."
- Wayne Dyer

"One small positive thought in the morning can change your whole day." –Unknown

These quotes remind us the importance of mental self-care, how our thoughts and mindset shape our reality, and how our attitude and perspective play a crucial role in our mental well-being. It also highlights the importance

# Social Self-Care

Social self-care is the practice of taking care of one's relationships in order to maintain overall health and happiness. It involves building and maintaining healthy relationships with friends, family, and community, and includes activities such as spending time with loved ones, practicing active listening and communication, and being vulnerable. By making social self-care a priority, individuals can improve their social connections, decrease feelings of loneliness and isolation, and increase their overall well-being.

Spending time with loved ones: Human beings are social animals and having healthy relationships is vital for overall well-being. Spending time with friends and family can provide support and help individuals feel more connected to others.

Active listening and communication: Effective communication and active listening can help individuals build deeper connections with others. It involves listening to others with an open mind and trying to understand their point of view.

Being vulnerable: Being vulnerable in relationships means opening up and sharing one's thoughts and feelings with others. It can be difficult, but it allows others to connect with you on a deeper level and can lead to stronger and more meaningful relationships.

Empathy: Being empathetic means trying to understand and share the feelings of others. It is an important aspect of social self-care as it can help individuals build strong relationships with others and improve their ability to connect with others.

Making time for others: Helping others can be a great way to feel good about oneself. It could be something as simple as doing a favor for a friend, volunteering or checking in on a loved one who may be going through a tough time.

It's important to remember that social self-care is not just about being in a romantic relationship but also about building and maintaining healthy relationships with friends, family and community.

It's important to find a routine that works for you, and to make it a regular part of your life. Whether it's spending an hour on the phone with a friend, going out to lunch with a loved one, or volunteering for a cause you're passionate about, the key is to find something that you enjoy and can stick to.

Incorporating social self-care into daily life can be challenging, but it is worth it. By making social self-care a priority, individuals can improve their social connections, decrease feelings of loneliness and isolation, and increase their overall well-being.

Here are a few quotes related to social self-care:

"Alone we can do so little; together we can do so much." - Helen Keller

"The greatest thing in the world is to know how to belong to oneself." - Michel de Montaigne

"The best way to cheer yourself is to try to cheer someone else up." - Mark Twain

"The greatest gift of life is friendship, and I have received it." - Hubert H. Humphrey

"Connection is why we're here; it is what gives purpose and meaning to our lives." - Brené Brown

"No one can make you feel inferior without your consent." - Eleanor Roosevelt

"Surround yourself with people who make you better, who lift you higher." –Unknown

"You are the average of the five people you spend the most time with." -Jim Rohn

"Friendship isn't about who you've known the longest. It's about who walked into your life and said "I'm here for you." – Unknown

"The greatest wealth is to live content with little." –Plato

These quotes remind us the importance of social self-care, how social connections are essential for our overall well-being, how being surrounded by positive people can have a positive impact on our well-being. It also highlights the importance of self-respect and self-worth.

# Spiritual Self-Care

Spiritual self-care is the practice of taking care of one's inner self in order to maintain overall health and happiness. It involves finding a sense of meaning, purpose and connection to something greater than oneself, and includes activities such as meditation, prayer, mindfulness, and connecting with nature. By making spiritual self-care a priority, individuals can improve their sense of well-being, find inner peace, and cultivate a deeper understanding of themselves and the world around them.

Meditation: Meditation is a practice that involves focusing the mind on a particular object, thought or activity to achieve a mentally clear and emotionally calm state. It is often used to reduce stress and anxiety and can also bring a sense of inner peace and tranquility.

Prayer: Prayer is a form of communication with a higher power and can bring a sense of connection to something greater than oneself. It is a way to express gratitude, seek guidance, and find inner peace.

Mindfulness: Mindfulness is the practice of being present in the moment, without judgment. It can also be used to connect with something greater than oneself and gain a deeper understanding of oneself and the world around us.

Connecting with nature: Spending time in nature can be a powerful way to connect with something greater than oneself. It can bring a sense of peace and tranquility and help individuals gain a greater appreciation for the natural world.

Self-reflection: Reflecting on one's inner self, values, beliefs, and purpose can help individuals gain a deeper understanding of themselves and their place in the world. This can include journaling, meditating, or talking with a spiritual advisor.

It's important to note that spiritual self-care may take different forms, depending on the individual and their beliefs. It can involve organized religion, or it can be a more personal and individual journey of self-discovery.

It's important to find a routine that works for you, and to make it a regular part of your life. Whether it's meditating for 10 minutes each morning, spending an hour in nature each week, or attending a religious service once a month, the key is to find something that you enjoy and can stick to.

Incorporating spiritual self-care into daily life can be challenging, but it is worth it. By making spiritual self-care a priority, individuals can improve their sense of well-being, find inner peace, and cultivate a deeper understanding of themselves and the world around them.

Here are a few quotes related to spiritual self-care:

"The quieter you become, the more you can hear." -Ram Dass

"Spirituality is not about religion, it's about the connection with something greater than ourselves."
– Unknown

"The more you know yourself, the less you are likely to get lost in the world." –Unknown

"The spiritual journey is the unlearning of fear and prejudices and the acceptance of love back in our hearts." -Marianne Williamson

"Spiritual growth is not about perfection; it's about becoming more of who we already are." – Unknown

"To be spiritual is to be constantly aware of the presence of the divine."
–Unknown

"The spiritual journey is the unlearning of fear and prejudices and the acceptance of love back in our hearts." -Marianne Williamson

"Spiritual growth is not a matter of learning new ideas, but of experiencing a new consciousness."
-Eckhart Tolle

"Spirituality is the connection to the divine, to something greater than ourselves, that gives us a sense of peace and meaning." –Unknown

"True spiritual growth is the ability to let go of things that no longer serve us." –Unknown

These quotes remind us the importance of spiritual self-care, how it is essential to have a connection to something greater than ourselves, how it can bring inner peace, and how it can help in personal growth, and self-discovery. It also highlights the importance of letting go of things that no longer serve us and the role of spirituality in personal growth.

# Financial Self-Care

Financial self-care is the practice of taking care of one's finances in order to maintain overall health and happiness. It involves developing healthy money habits, creating a budget, saving for the future, and managing debt. By making financial self-care a priority, individuals can improve their financial well-being, reduce stress and anxiety, and create a more stable and secure future.

Creating a budget: A budget is a plan for how to allocate your money. It can help individuals keep track of their income and expenses, and make sure they are saving enough for the future and not overspending.

Saving for the future: Saving money is important for long-term financial security. It can help individuals achieve their financial goals and provide a safety net in case of emergency.

Managing debt: Managing debt is an important part of financial self-care. It involves creating a plan to pay off debt and make sure that it doesn't accumulate.

Investing: Investing money can help individuals grow their wealth over time. It's important to learn about different investment options, such as stocks, bonds, and real estate, and choose the one that aligns with your financial goals and risk tolerance.

Financial Planning: Having a plan for your financial future can give peace of mind and help individuals make decisions that align with their goals.

It's important to note that financial self-care is not only about earning more money, it's also about learning how to manage it better and create sustainable habits.

It's important to find a routine that works for you and to make it a regular part of your life. Whether it's setting aside a specific day each week to review your budget, or automating your savings, the key is to find something that you can stick to.

Incorporating financial self-care into daily life can be challenging, but it is worth it. By making financial self-care a priority, individuals can improve their financial well-being, reduce stress and anxiety, and create a more stable and secure future.

Here are a few quotes related to financial self-care:

"Money is not the most important thing in the world. Love is. Fortunately, I love money." - Jackie Mason

"It's not how much money you make, but how much money you keep, how hard it works for you, and how many generations you keep it for." - Robert Kiyosaki

"Wealth is not about having a lot of money; it's about having a lot of options." – Chris Rock

"The habit of saving is itself an education; it fosters every virtue, teaches self-denial, cultivates the sense of order, trains to forethought, and so broadens the mind." - T.T. Munger

"The biggest mistake people make is not trying to make a living doing what they most enjoy." - Malcolm Forbes

"The love of money is the root of all evil." – 1 Timothy 6:10

"The stock market is a device for transferring money from the impatient to the patient." - Warren Buffett

"I will tell you the secret to getting rich on Wall Street. You try to be greedy when others are fearful. And you try to be fearful when others are greedy." -Warren Buffett

"Frugality includes all the other virtues" - Cicero

In addition to the above quotes, financial self-care also involves setting financial goals, having an emergency fund, paying off debt, and regularly reviewing and adjusting one's financial plan. Furthermore, it is important to have a good understanding of financial basics and staying informed about personal finance. By practicing financial self-care, individuals are better equipped to handle financial challenges and make informed decisions about their money.

# Occupational Self-Care

Occupational self-care is the practice of taking care of one's well-being in the workplace in order to maintain overall health and happiness. It involves setting boundaries, managing stress, setting and achieving goals, and seeking support. By making occupational self-care a priority, individuals can improve their job satisfaction, increase their productivity, and reduce burnout.

Setting boundaries: Setting boundaries in the workplace means being clear about what you are willing to do and what you are not willing to do, in order to ensure that your own needs and priorities are being met. This can include setting limits on work hours, taking breaks, and saying no to tasks that are not part of your job responsibilities.

Managing stress: Stress is a common experience in the workplace, so it's important to have strategies for dealing with it. This can include exercise, mindfulness, relaxation techniques and effective time management.

Setting and achieving goals: Setting and achieving goals can help increase job satisfaction and a sense of accomplishment in the workplace. This can include setting small, achievable goals and taking steps towards larger, long-term goals.

Seeking support: Seeking support from colleagues, supervisors, or a therapist can be helpful in managing the demands of the workplace. This can include seeking feedback, asking for help when needed, and joining a support group.

Work-Life balance: Striving for a balance between work and other aspects of life can reduce burnout and improve overall well-being. This can include setting specific hours for work, scheduling time for leisure activities, and making sure to disconnect from work when not on the clock.

It's important to remember that occupational self-care is not just about the hours spent at work but also about how one manages and balances the demands of their job with the rest of their life.

It's important to find a routine that works for you, and to make it a regular part of your life. Whether it's setting a specific time each day to review your goals, or taking a 15-minute break each hour to stretch and relax, the key is to find something that you can stick to.

Incorporating occupational self-care into daily life can be challenging, but it is worth it. By making occupational self-care a priority, individuals can improve their job satisfaction, increase their productivity, and reduce burnout.

Here are a few quotes related to occupational self-care:

"Choose a job you love, and you will never have to work a day in your life." –Confucius

"Your work is going to fill a large part of your life, and the only way to be truly satisfied is to do what you believe is great work. And the only way to do great work is to love what you do." -Steve Jobs

"Happiness is not something ready made. It comes from your own actions." -Dalai Lama

"Do what you love, and success will follow." –Unknown

"The best way to predict the future of your career is to create it." - Abraham Lincoln

"The true test of a career is to be able to be content, even proud, that you succeeded through your own endeavors without leaving a trail of casualties in your wake." - Robert Reich

"Choose a job you love, and you will never have to work a day in your life." – Confucius

"The best way to find yourself is to lose yourself in the service of others." -Mahatma Gandhi

"Work to become, not to acquire." -
Elbert Hubbard

"Your work is going to fill a large part of your life. The only way to be truly satisfied is to do what you believe is great work. And the only way to do great work is to love what you do." -Steve Jobs

These quotes remind us the importance of finding a job that aligns with our values and passions, how it is essential to find the job that make us truly satisfied, how it is essential to find the job that we love to do and how it will affect us positively in our overall well-being, and also the importance of balancing work with the rest of life, and the impact of work on our well-being.

# Conclusion and Next Steps

Self-care is an essential aspect of overall health and well-being. It involves taking care of one's physical, emotional, mental, social, spiritual, financial and occupational well-being in order to maintain overall health and happiness.

In this book, we have discussed the various aspects of self-care and provided examples of activities and strategies that can be used to incorporate self-care into daily life. We have also discussed the importance of finding a routine that works for you and making self-care a regular part of your life.

While reading this book you may have identified areas in which you would like to improve your self-care routine or learned something new, now it's time to take action. You can start by setting specific goals for yourself and creating a plan to achieve them. It's important to be realistic and patient with yourself, remember that change takes time.

It's also important to remember that self-care is an ongoing process and it's okay to adjust your plan as needed. Take some time to reflect on your progress and evaluate what is working and what is not. If you find that you're struggling to maintain your self-care routine, don't be afraid to reach out for support from friends, family, or a professional.

Self-care is not just about taking care of yourself, but also about taking care of the people around you. Be kind and compassionate with yourself, and extend that same kindness and compassion to others. Remember that self-care is not just a one-time action, it's a daily practice.

In conclusion, self-care is a holistic approach to taking care of oneself. It's not just about physical or mental health but also an important practice to maintain overall well-being. Remember to take time for yourself, prioritize your well-being, and make self-care a regular part of your life. Remember that self-care can be challenging, but it's worth it.